R.A.T. FI(

Combat Secrets of the World's Deadliest Fighters

Rapid Assault Tactics

Paul Vunak

Published by S.P. in agreement with Spy Briefing, LLC.

Important Publishers Note

This publication is designed to provide accurate and authoritative information in regard to the subject matter covered. If legal advice or any type of assistance is needed, please seek the services of a competent professional. This book, published by the Spy Briefing, LLC, is for informational purposes only. All technical information, instruction, and advice, reflect the beliefs of Spy Briefing, LLC and are intended as informational only. This book is not intended to serve as a replacement for professional instruction. You agree to indemnify, and hold harmless the Spy Briefing, LLC from any and all such claims and damages as a result of reading this book, which is for informational purposes only.

"THIS IS DEDICATED
TO MY SIFU
DAN INOSANTO
AND TO THE MEMORY OF
BRUCE LEE."

-PAUL VUNAK

Table of Contents

Preface
Anatomy of a Street Fight

"If you want to understand the truth in martial arts, to see any fight clearly, you must throw away the notion of styles or schools, prejudices, likes and dislikes, and so forth. Then, your mind will cease all conflict and come to rest. In this silence, you will see totally and freshly." - **Bruce Lee**

Let's first discuss and define the meaning behind “anatomy of a street fight.” What is a street fight? If we were to take a worldwide survey and ask, "Who is the best fighter on the planet?" it would quickly become obvious the difference in perception.

The average American would probably pick his favorite heavyweight boxer, perhaps Mike Tyson (however, the question was not "who is the best boxer?") The average Filipino would probably answer, “Floro Villabrille” (a legendary stick/blade master, but the question was not "who is the best weapons fighter?")

Ask the question in Brazil, and the answer might be "Rickson Gracie" or “Rigan Machado” (however, the question was not "who is the best ground fighter?") So, I ask again, what exactly is a street fight? It is any random act of violence, period!

While this definition includes kicking, punching, stick and knife fighting, and ground fighting, it does not preclude two-on-one, three-on-one, four-on-two, pinching, biting, eye gouging, firearms, car jackings, and all-out riots.

This book is not about tradition, it is not about styles or systems. It is not about sports or tournaments, and certainly not about rules.

My objective is to introduce the "rigid rod of reality." Violence cannot be contained within a neat little package. It is not to be taken lightly and certainly not to be romanticized.

This book clarifies some issues that have previously been clouded, sparks some questions that should be asked, and ultimately fills in a hole and completes the puzzle.

Chapter 1: No-Holds-Barred Tournaments Are Not Street Fights

The last several years of martial arts have seen more growth and progress than the previous fifty, because of the insurgence of the many no-holds-barred tournaments occurring worldwide.

My respect and admiration for these warriors goes beyond words. They are among the toughest, most well-conditioned athletes on the planet. We see the quality of fighters improving each year. These fighters are becoming more complete every day.

Punchers and kickers are learning to grapple, and grapplers are slowly learning to punch and kick. Being well-rounded and multidimensional are no longer just trendy ideas, but downright necessities.

Although they may not realize it, these fighters are truly harvesting the seeds that were planted by Bruce Lee and Dan Inosanto in the 1970s.

All one has to do is pick up The Tao of Jeet Kune Do, and it becomes obvious that the principles and concepts the two discovered are being implemented to a "T."

Complicating matters further is that many of these scenarios usually end up mutating.

Now things become exponentially more difficult. By mutating, I mean changing from one scenario to another within the same fight.

For example, the altercation may start off one-on-one standing up and then go to the ground. If another individual jumps in we have a two-on-one fight.

Then perhaps two more people enter the equation, giving us a three-on-two situation. At this point, someone might grab a pipe and now this has turned into a weapons fight.

In retaliation, someone else may grab a blade. Now the scenario has changed to a knife fight. These mutations could potentially be endless.

The first thing that comes to mind when talking about being a streetfighter is that one must be prepared for a mass-attack scenario and with all types of weapons - sticks, knives, etc. (According to law enforcement statistics, eight out of ten streetlights involve weapons!)

The next attribute in our quest to become a complete streetfighter is keeping a cool head while these mutations occur. Controlling one's emotions is one of the most essential aspects of a fight. There are moments in the midst of battle where one must "turn on" his killer instinct.

There are other moments when controlling the emotions means relaxing and breathing. This is when you are in the moment, I like to call the "Fog of War."

If one is not highly trained in all areas of combat and a scenario occurs in which you have never experienced, panic occurs and controlling your emotions is impossible.

Most people in martial arts are too specialized in their "way" of fighting. For example, if a person's "way" is stick fighting, and he loses his stick, he would certainly be in trouble.

If a person's "way" is kickboxing and he ends up on the ground, he would also be in trouble.

If a person's "way" is ground fighting and he has to fight more than one person, he also would be in trouble. This is why Bruce Lee espoused the rather esoteric axiom of "using no way as way."

Some schools out there are "eclectic" in that they train in many of the aforementioned areas.

However, the problem is that they have a tendency to simply compartmentalize these areas. They have a 4 p.m. stick class, a 5 p.m. kickboxing class, a 6 p.m. ground fighting class, and so on.

This sort of training does not promote flowing and adapting to the various possible mutations of a street fight.

In boxing, this would be akin to having a 4 p.m. jab class, a 5 p.m. cross class and a 6 p.m. hook class.

Having classes compartmentalized like this is not in itself a bad thing, provided you follow Guro Dan Inosanto's methodology - have one class at your school that combines everything. Guro Dan has always taught me that you will train the way you fight and fight the way you train.

Chapter 2: Guide to Training JKD Attributes

20 of the most important ways to train for the "anything-can-happen" street fight

Attributes and Training Methods

1. Awareness
   - Definition: To see the opponent's intentions.
   - Training Method: Knife sparring, mixed sparring (one side uses jab only, the other uses all tools).

2. Sensitivity
   - Definition: To feel the opponent's intentions.
   - Training Method: Hubud (Filipino energy drill), Chi Sao, etc.

3. Proper Mental Attitude
   - Definition: Combination of calm, killer instinct, and confidence.
   - Training Method: Full-contact training (with loud abusive language), use of vivid imagery during training.

4. Body Mechanics
   - Definition: Knowing how and where to position the body at all times, using no wasted motion.
   - Training Method: Weapons training of all types (forces one to exaggerate and emphasize body mechanics).

5. Strength
   - Definition: Ability to overwhelm an opponent through manipulation.
   - Training Method: Weight training, wrestling, isometrics, swimming, gymnastics, surfing.

6. Footwork
   - Definition: Putting oneself where one needs to be at all times by shuffling forward and back, sidestepping and circling.
   - Training Method: Knife sparring (long range), empty-hand sparring (jab only), jumping rope, running bleachers.

7. Speed
   - Definition: Perception of initiation and performance of an action.
   - Training Method: Break any motion into three equal parts (from chambered position to impact) and work each part separately. Also stick sparring.

8. Power
    - Definition: Combination of strength and speed (ability to use your strength quickly).
    - Training Method: Heavy bag work, isometrics, wrestling, throwing shot put, full-contact sparring (w/proper gear).

9. Timing
    - Definition: Ability to launch an attack at the proper moment.
    - Training Method: Knife sparring (decreasing speed by 50 percent increases need for timing by 50 percent).

10. Coordination
    - Definition: Performing a movement with efficiency, ease and balance.
    - Training Method: Double-stick training, focus gloves, cross-training in any physical sport; repetition of desired motion.

11. Balance
    - Definition: Correct body alignment during motion (controlling one's center of gravity).
    - Training Method: Most physical sports, especially surfing, water and snow skiing, high kicking, gymnastics.

12. Spatial Relationships
    - Definition: Control over distances.
    - Training Method: Mixed-weapons sparring using weapons of different ranges (e.g., staff vs. single stick, double-stick vs. knife, etc.).

13. Agility
    - Definition: Being light on one's feet with limberness and quickness.
    - Training Method: Gymnastics, knife sparring, handball.

14. Stamina
    - Definition: Combined endurance and wind.
    - Training Method: Wrestling, Thai boxing drills, heavy bag work, running, sparring, high kicking.

15. Conditioning
    - Definition: Taking punishment to hands, stomach, thighs, skins.
    - Training Method: Mook Jong (wooden dummy), Thai boxing drills, shin kicks to heavy bag, straw pad.

16. Killer Instinct

17. Rhythm

• Definition: Deals with faking, cadence breaks, changing tempos, etc.
• Training Method: Double-sticks, conga playing, dancing, speed bag work.

18. Precision
    • Definition: Accuracy and exactness in the projection of force.
    • Training Method: Hitting a paper dangling from a string, hitting small targets (use a felt pen) on the heavy bag.

19. Explosiveness
    • Definition: Relaying destructiveness in a sudden manner.
    • Training Method: Wrestling, weight training (clean and jerk), heavy bag, and tackle football.

20. Flow
    • Definition: Combination of awareness and sensitivity; uninterrupted concentration.
    • Training Method: Stick training (counter drills), empty-hand drills in which one continues through a series of movements without stopping.

A GUIDE TO TRAINING JEET KUNE DO ATTRIBUTES

We have already established that adapting during the many potential transitions is critical. Therefore, to prepare yourself for the street, your training has to mimic all potential mutations that might possibly occur.

For example, start your practice session by stick fighting, then drop your stick, pull out a blade, and continue the match knife fighting. Throw down the blade and continue with kickboxing. Then enter into trapping range, implementing headbutts, elbows, and knees.

Next, take the fight to the ground and kick into Brazilian Jiu-Jitsu. Look for the appropriate time to use Kina Mutay (uninterrupted biting and eye gouging).

At this point you could throw another student into the fray - instantly come to your feet and continue the fight as a mass attack. This entire round should flow with no interruptions.

Training in this manner emphasizes some of the most vital attributes for a street fight:

Adapting and controlling the emotions during transitions. I would like to re-emphasize the incredible respect I have for the competitors of NHB tournaments. Their conditioning and focus are at an uncommon level.

In fact, they are so focused that this could be detrimental in an actual street fight. I have borne witness to this firsthand. Indulge me for a moment while I share with you an experience from a day many years ago in 1990.

It was a typical Friday afternoon. My partner, Thomas Cruse, and I had just finished working with one of the Navy SEAL teams. As tradition would have it, the guys would take us out to their favorite hangout to have a few beers.

Our motley crew consisted of three Navy men, Thomas, and myself. Our three buddies were all former heavyweight wrestlers of Olympic caliber, with the approximate build of a Mark Coleman or a Mark Kerr.

When we arrived at the bar, it looked like something out of a movie: A stereotypical biker bar. My visceral response was to say, "Guys, let's just go home ... this place looks like a fight waiting to happen."

But I knew I had Thomas on one side and I glanced over at my three buddies (which translated into about 900 pounds of beef) and thought to myself, "So what - if we fight, we fight." (That was my mentality in those days.)

That was Scene One. Scene Two. A couple of hours later, Thomas is pulling a typical Tom Cruise in The Color of Money, running the pool table and irritating bikers right and left.

Finally, the whole bar goes into what one could only call a "huddle," and out steps the kingpin biker, a pool player from Hell.

Scene Three. Cruse now has a few hundred dollars of this guy's money, my wrestling buddies are at the other side of the bar talking to some women, and I am grimly assessing the situation. I'm thinking ... "I've seen this movie before."

At this point, the two pool players are down to their last game and Thomas has a straight-in shot on the 9-ball to win the match. Instead of simply making the shot and going home a winner, Thomas looks over at me, makes some wisecrack about, "Einstein taught me this," and makes a triple bank and buries it.

To say that the already volatile situation had reached critical mass would be a slight understatement. We now had about 20 bikers against the five of us. Fists, bottles, and chairs started flying.

The three heavyweight wrestlers, all in unison like some synchronized swim show, focused in on one guy apiece, and, in a state of rage took them straight to the ground. This left Thomas and me to deal with the rest of the bar!

This was one of the worst beatings I have ever taken. In fact, all five of us ended up in the hospital. I personally got the worst of the deal and spent four days in intensive care.

It is important to emphasize here that each one of those wrestlers would have done exceptionally well in any no-holds-barred tournament.

Here is the moral to the story: This wasn't a no-holds-barred tournament. This was the street. In the street, you have to be prepared to take on multiple attackers and you can't just focus on one person like the Navy guys did, leaving the rest of the bar to me and Thomas.

Chapter 3: Rapid Assault Tactics: The Navy SEAL Fighting System

There is so much contained within the vessel that is Jeet Kune Do, it would take a person an entire lifetime to experience it all.

It has been my personal goal (during more than 30 years of teaching) to put the most functional aspects of JKD into a format that can be easily absorbed by the average individual.

I originally developed this program for our East Coast Navy SEALs (they have so little time to allocate to martial arts, I was forced to streamline the most important elements into a formula that could be learned very quickly).

Subsequently, I discovered that many other government agencies have enjoyed this program as well.

The important thing to remember is to have a game plan. In the world of professional sports, athletes spend surprisingly little time on their game skills (like shooting baskets, catching passes, etc.), and more time on developing, learning, and running specific plays.

A National Football League coach would never send his team into the Super Bowl without a game plan. You should have the same approach to self-defense. Possessing skills and techniques alone aren't enough, you need to have an agenda.

The first few moments of an attack, when the adrenaline starts pumping and your heart starts racing, is not the appropriate time to try to formulate a defensive strategy!

You need a game plan that you can practice ahead of time so in the event of a crisis, you will be able to instinctively do what it takes to survive.

OUR GAME PLAN: THE RAT SYSTEM
(Rapid Assault Tactics)

Angelo Dundee, trainer of the legendary Muhammad Ali, once proclaimed, "The first-est with the most-est is the best-est!" He understood that perhaps the single most important attribute one could possess in an all-out street fight is overwhelming one's opponent.

And by "overwhelming," I do not mean just physically blasting through someone, but overwhelming him emotionally as well. This means we are going to rattle this opponent - cause him to flinch, shut his eyes, cover up, and perhaps turn away. Once this occurs, the rest of the fight gets exponentially easier.

The difficulty of any street fight lies in that zone where both fighters are trading blows. This is when you are most vulnerable, especially if your opponent is larger and stronger.

The ability to “turn on” a sudden burst of firepower, assaulting your opponent as rapidly as possible, is an indispensable asset.

The principles of Rapid Assault Tactics come directly from Bruce Lee. Although he never formally promoted this systematic approach to an altercation (it just came naturally to him), we have only to examine his tactics when he considered a fight to be serious to see these principles in action.

One of Bruce Lee's greatest assets was the way he began an encounter in a seemingly complete state of relaxation and then suddenly erupted in movement almost too fast for the eye to see.

In a fight, Bruce would intercept his opponent before he could even finish launching his blow.

This interception would typically be a quick shot to the eyes, knees or groin and would prevent any trading of blows. He would then follow up with a modified version of Wing Chun's straight blast - a series of straight vertical punches rolling down the opponent's centerline.

This happened so quickly the opponent ended up flapping his arms and backpedaling furiously, sometimes on one leg. Bruce jokingly used to refer to the helpless recipient of the powerful straight blast as a “wounded crane.”

When a person is on the receiving end of a straight blast, one thing is certain: He has no base and no balance, which are two mandatory factors for any style to be effective.

The art of Wing Chun was developed by a woman, no doubt smaller and not as strong as her male counterparts. The underlying premise of using Wing Chun is that you are fighting a bigger, stronger opponent. Trading kicks and punches is clearly not the ideal strategy.

The best way to mitigate the size differential is to apply forward pressure to get your opponent backpedaling. Picture taking a worldwide tour to find the best representative of each and every martial art style.

Imagine finding the best Tae Kwon Do person, the best Kenpo Karate practitioner or the best kung-fu sifu, for example. Each individual has a style of fighting and each possesses his respective attributes.

Now, picture these people running backward, frantically trying to stay upright and getting out of the way of fists flying at their faces. Can you then imagine these people trying to pull off their techniques?

It is an immutable principle that is not affected by style or skill level: Once someone is running backward, he is transformed from a martial artist into a simple pedestrian!

It's safe to say that no one practices his art while running backward; however, before you start a new "backward training" program, remember that it's not the reversed direction, but rather the lack of base and balance, that renders the straight blast recipient ineffective.

It's ironic that most people's perception of how Bruce Lee fought has undoubtedly been fostered by his movies.

On film, his theatrical Jeet Kune Do was incredibly fun, fancy, and highly entertaining. In reality, Bruce's movement was simple, economical and direct. Dan Inosanto has said, "Every fight that I have ever seen Bruce in when he was serious, he would straight blast."

After Bruce died in 1973, the responsibility of keeping JKD alive and growing (never static) was conferred upon Dan.

Although we read in the Tao of Jeet Kune Do about the effectiveness of headbutts, knees, and elbows, the truth is that all of Bruce's fights ended right after the straight blast! Because of his superior attributes, he could execute the blast so flawlessly that he never needed to follow up with an elbow or a knee strike.

Obviously, there are few others in this world who possess similar abilities; most of us need everything that Bruce and Dan discovered!

As Dan grew in his pursuit of the Filipino martial arts, he discovered how incredibly functional and destructive, and how natural it was to finish off the straight blast with a barrage of elbows, headbutts, and knees.

With the addition of these tools to the JKD cocktail, Bruce's already super effective art became even better.

AN OVERVIEW OF THE FIGHT

I have broken down a fight into three phases, each of equal importance. I will explain what each phase is and the methods for implementing each phase's tactics.

First, we have to enter. If we do not enter in a street fight, we cannot get into the most lethal range to terminate the fight - where we can use our headbutts, knees and elbows. Everything starts from the entry.

Most martial artists kick and punch or grapple. When they're in long range they're going to be throwing bombs at us. We absolutely don't want to trade bombs with people, it will not work, especially if our opponent is larger and stronger.

It doesn't matter what style he practices - hard style, soft style, circular, linear - we cannot trade bombs. To enter, we have to either intercept or destroy. An interception and a destruction have one thing in common: inflicting instantaneous pain.

Once our opponent has been subjected to the pain of an interception or destruction, we then go into pressure. Pressure is possibly the most important facet of our game plan.

The pressure comes from the art of Wing Chun and borrows from a technique called the

Jik Chun Choy or straight blast. As I just mentioned, one of Bruce Lee's biggest revelations was that once your opponent is running backward, he has lost all ability to hurt you.

Now that our opponent feels this incredible pressure (the 50-yard dash down his centerline), it is time to terminate the fight.

This is accomplished by using the three most barbaric tools on the human body: The knees, the elbows and the headbutt, which will render an attacker useless.

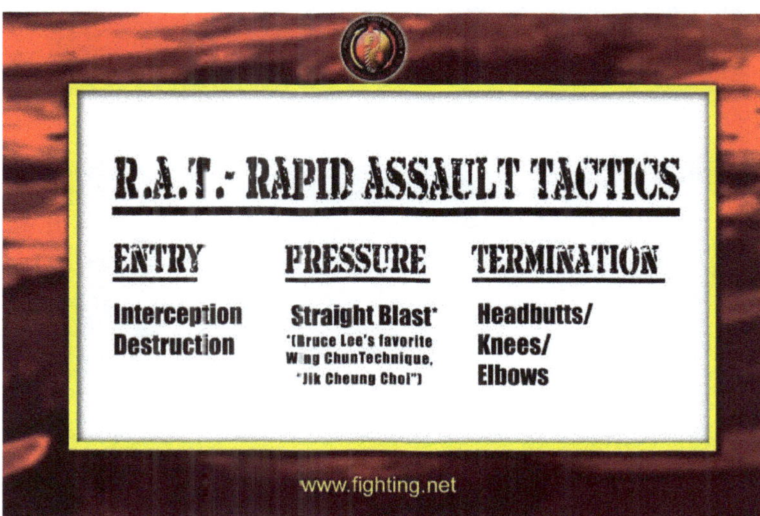

Now that you have an overview of the whole game plan, let's look at each phase in greater detail.

The Author: Paul Vunak with Members of SEAL Team 6 (DevGru)

The Author: Paul Vunak training fight termination, with SEAL Team 6 (DevGru)

The 3 Phases of the R.A.T.

Phase One: ENTRY and DESTRUCTIONS

As you know, phase One is the ENTRY and let's start with destructions. We will first cover destructions on the upper half and then the lower half of the body. We can then combine them.

Training Tip: You always need to have your training partner trying to hit you when they are throwing punches at you. Don't throw punches in front of the face, but actually go through your punches and try to make contact, this is why we put on gloves.

This way you will not be wondering if your techniques really work, you always know if it really works because you are trying to hit each other. We really try to wrestle if we go to the ground.

If you are really applying the correct pressure, there is not much difference between your training and the street fight.

Many people think, I have never been in a street fight, maybe I need to go out and get into street fights to make this work, NO! If your training is realistic enough, you don't have to do that.

Destructions for Punches

R.A.T. elbow posture

The Elbow Form: The nose and the tip of your elbow must line up. You move around while maintaining this position, with footwork, while your opponent throws punches at you. Elbow destructions are no good if there is no footwork.

Review: He throws punches at you and your hands are up with impeccable form and his punches collide with your elbows. If he walks up to you or you are sitting in a bar, and you see him approaching you from the corner of your eye, BAM!

Intercept him with an elbow or eye jab, and then on to the straight blast and termination phases of the fight.

Destructions for Kicks:

Let's start with lowline kicks. The knees cover the low-line, the elbows cover the high-line for most kicks. When your elbows and knees meet, you have an air tight defense. This is your cocoon of elbows and knees.

Training Tip: You have to protect your face. Just because I am doing kick destructions, I don't want to drop my hands, because if he throws a punch, I don't want to then have to raise my arms up and have my elbows in the correct position.

Your elbows must be occupying the highline at all times. So, your hands are up, the elbows are in front of your face, and any punch that comes in, BAM it runs right into your elbow.

Low-Line Kicks:

Now with the low-line kicking, you are up on your toes, with your elbows up, and as soon as something comes you just pick up your leg and point the knee at it.

Any kick that comes to the frontal area, point the knee inward.

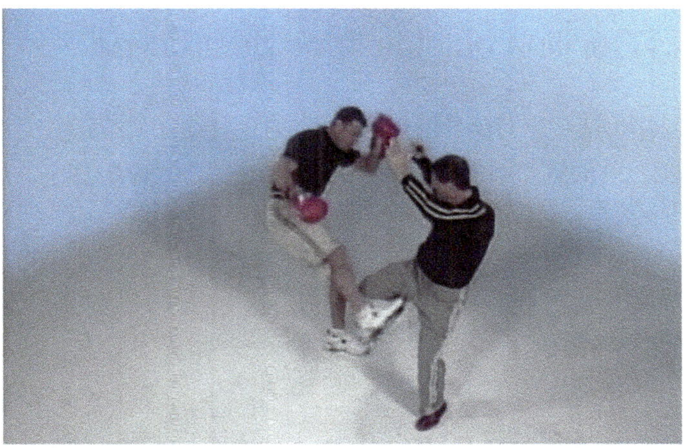

R.A.T. lowline inside knee destruction

R.A.T. lowline outside knee destruction

Any kick that comes to the rear like a "Thai" shot, I just point the knee outward.

R.A.T. low line frontal knee destruction

Any kick that comes in from the rear like a side kick, just point the knee forward.

Training Tip: Make sure your training partner throws one line of kicks at a time, so that you can execute the correct form and posture before moving on to the next one.

Don't put in punches, don't put in high kicks. Just get up on your toes, and work one set of attacks at a time. Make sure to keep your elbows up and maintain impeccable form, while destroying the kicks.

The destructions must be augmented with movement. You are using the boxers footwork, the Thai boxers form by keeping your elbows up, you are using Kali or Escrima for the low line destructions by moving the knee.

High-Line Kicks:

Interestingly enough, on the high-line, somebody can spend 20 years working high kicks and it could take that long. You could be in a Korean Art, Tae-Kwon Do, Karate or the French Art of Savate. It takes a long time to master those kicks.

There is one move you can use that will counter 20 years of high kicking. Just raise your leg straight up to the groin.

It doesn't matter which foot, which high kick, round or spin, it makes no difference. Get your head out of the way and just raise your leg straight up to the groin.

R.A.T. highline groin kick counter

So, if it is a towline kick you just raise your knee and point it in or out, depending on frontal, inside or outside.

If it is a high-line, and you might have thought it was low, all you have to do is extend your foot and hit the groin.

Training Tip: Make sure that your elbows are in front of your face. If he kicks really fast, you want to make sure the kick runs into your elbows, and not your head.

What you will find common in all destructions is that the minute a strike comes, it is instantly destroyed. The minute a kick comes it is instantly destroyed. This is not a block and go type of system.

In the traditional world, it usually takes about 15 or 20 years to learn how to block strikes properly. You start out as an amateur boxer and then your work your way into the pros.

You slip, bob, weave, duck, parry, and there is a whole world of timing issues and line familiarization and stamina and footwork. All of those attributes come into play when you try to duke it out with somebody.

Conversely, if you are not in that mode, and if you just want to put your hands up and they hit you, it takes 2 or 3 days and you can accomplish the same thing.

INTERCEPTIONS:

We make a cocoon of elbows and knees protecting us when the opponent is punching or kicking at us. If the opponent does not punch, and chooses to walk up to us we use interceptions.

When we intercept, we think of the four circles (or four balls) - Eyes and the groin. You just see four circles coming at you, no muscles no big tattoos, just four circles.

Some people like to walk up to you and get right in your face and talk. Before they get up into your face, I highly recommend that you hit them and simply don't stop hitting until they are done talking.

Sometimes people will cock the arm back, take a big wind up and, “boom” we take an eye jab interception.

As soon as you see the fight about to start, hit first and keep on hitting. Depending on your position, you can intercept by kicking to the groin or eye jabbing the eyes.

R.A.T. eye jab

After the interception, we complete the R.A.T. program by applying pressure with the straight blast and then terminating the fight with head-butts, knees, and elbows.

Phase Two: Pressure, the most important part of the R.A.T.

The pressure is called a Straight Blast. The more important criteria than having the "Perfect Wing Chun" form, is that you are applying:

A. Pressure on your opponent.
B. Pressure with straight punches

These are the only two criteria. It doesn't really matter if your punches are rolling perfectly or coming in a flurry of jab, cross, jab.

R.A.T. straight blast Wing Chun

Training Tip: Before you do the blast, we need to look at the footwork. If you are not moving around prior to the blast, your blast will not work.

You can't start from some kind of a stance, and think you are going to chase some guy with punches, because he will get out of the way or duck under you and take you to the ground.

Straight Blast Drill: Shrimping Footwork

Pick up a stick and swat it at your partner's stomach. Feed horizontal strikes and force your partner to stay up on his toes, keep on perpetually moving, and most importantly, it teaches your partner to stay at the correct distance.

The correct distance in fighting is not to stand two feet apart and square off. You can't do interceptions or destructions from this position. That is what you see in sport fighting.

You need to start out in long range and then blast down his center. You can't square off in the middle, in a range where you can both hit each other.

After Shrimping (hollowing out your mid-section) return with the blast. Partner A feeds the horizonal strikes using a stick, to partner B, and then B shrimps out, and then returns with the blast. The feeder partner A, must run back immediately after feeding the stick strikes, so that your training partner is forced to chase you.

You are trying to develop this incredible forward pressure, this blitz, right down somebody's centerline. But it has to be timed properly.

A jab, cross, and a jab, or three rolling punches, and make your partner chase you. If you just stand there, after feeding, your partner will not develop the correct forward pressure. A blast without footwork will not work.

Everyone looks the same when they are flailing their arms and running backwards.

R.A.T. straight blast drill chase

Everybody is basically a pedestrian when they are running backwards. It takes your skill away. So, what we want to do after our entry, after we have caused them pain, we want to take their skill away, we want to nullify martial artists by applying pressure.

Now this person is flailing backwards, whatever they were, they are not, and we are going to take them out of commission.

We are going to terminate the fight with a headbutt, the knees, and the elbows.

When you slam the top of your head into somebody's face, they don't look the same. It is not like a punch. It is not like anything you have ever seen. There is a reason why headbutts are not allowed in any Mixed Martial Arts tournament.

No tournament allows knees to the groin and there is a reason for that. If the UFC allowed this stuff, the fight would be over in a second or two. You could have a large man defeated by a smaller man, just like that. A thumb to the eye, a knee to the groin and it's over.

Phase 3: Termination - Elbows, Knees, and Headbutts

The Thai Clinch.

Training Tip: Anytime you grab your opponent's head in training, make sure that his head is held straight back and he is not leaning forward.

If his neck is not stiff and is soft, both of you will collide heads when you headbutt and you are going to hate life.

As long as he has his head back, you can apply all of your moves, with correct body mechanics, and also ensure the safety of your partner.

R.A.T. Thai Clinch

So, you have destroyed a punch, you are mowing him down with straight punches, you leap up and grab the Thai Clinch.

At this moment, you can take the eye gouge (thumb in the eye), headbutt and elbow. Then you can continue with elbows and knees to the groin. You can do this drill as hardcore or as relaxed as you want.

You can put a helmet on and you can really do it or you can do it like a demo.

R.A.T. Drill:

Partner A, feeds punches on the high line, you keep an air tight defense and then destroy the punch, cause pain, and initiate the blast.

Leap up and grab the neck, and then HKE (heads, knees, elbows.)

Training Tip: start off slow, and move your way through the program and adjust your intensity for what you need.

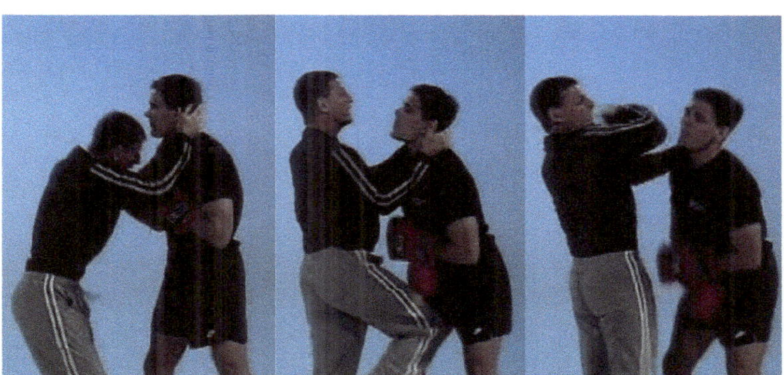

R.A.T. elbow destruction

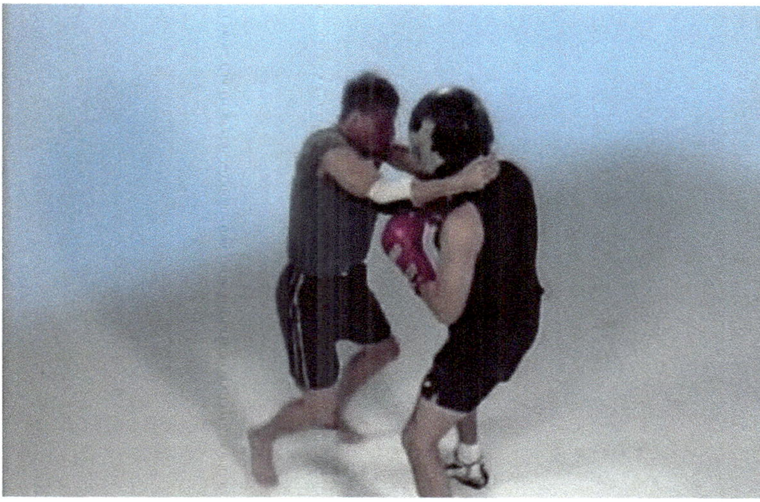

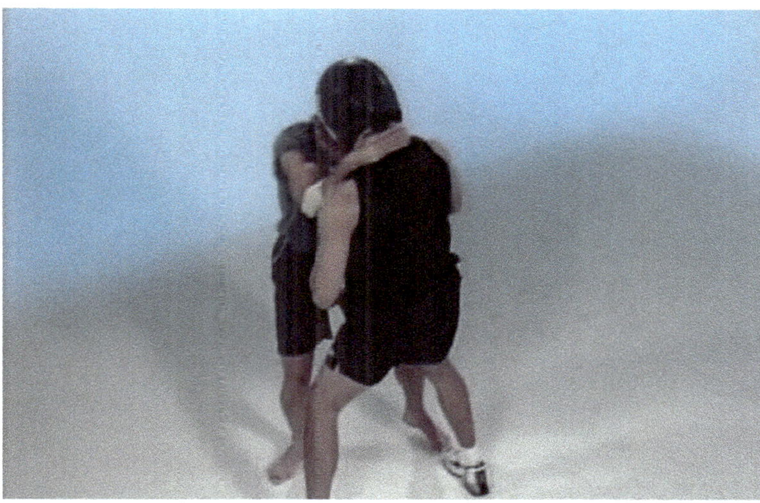

R.A.T. headbutt drilling

R.A.T. knee drilling

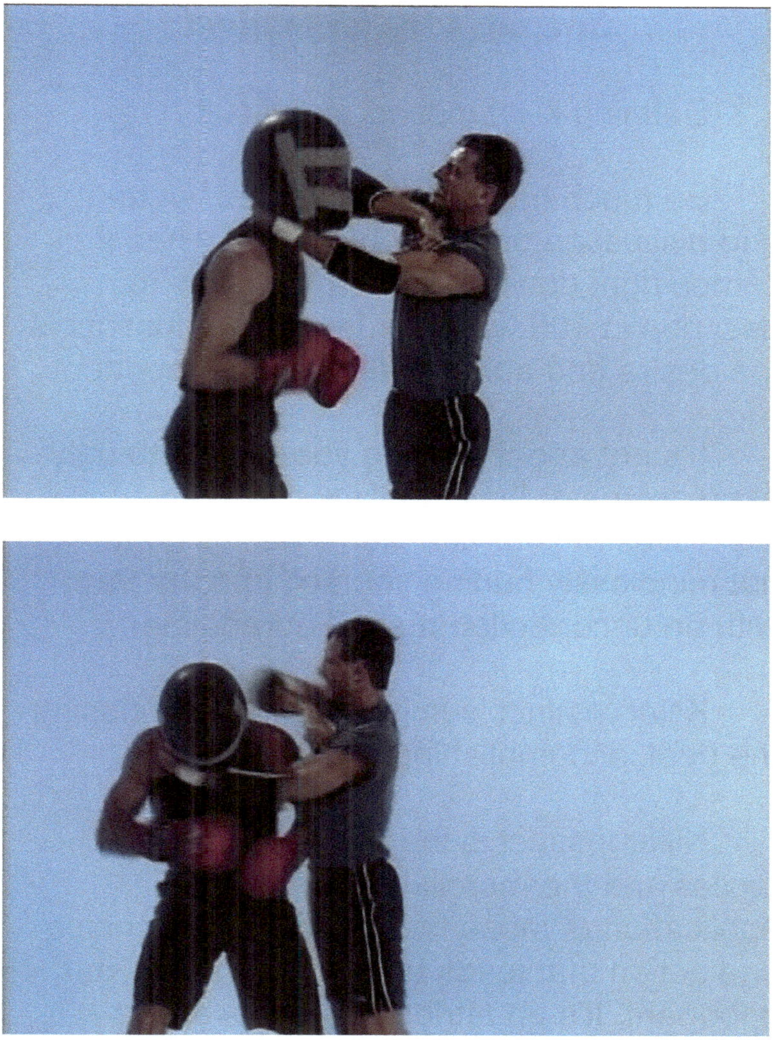

R.A.T. elbow drilling

Chapter 4: Killer Instinct

Defining killer instinct is difficult.

So much has been postulated, written, and discussed on the subject. But when it comes right down to it, it's impossible to describe in 100 words or less. Killer Instinct is the desire and ability to finish your opponent.

It's not about twisting your face into ugly expressions or how loudly you scream expletives at your attacker. And it is certainly not mindlessly hurling yourself into the fray with an uncontrolled rush of adrenaline.

Killer Instinct is finishing the race, closing the deal, accomplishing the mission.

Killer instinct is the correct choice of tactics and the merciless, relentless application of those tactics. It is every choice and action that leads to the downfall of your opponent. It's an attribute, but it is also a mentality.

Firm-gripped control over our most intense emotions is a hallmark of killer instinct. If we are to fully realize the maximum potential of our killer instinct, we cannot be a slave to our emotions.

Think of any predator and the manner in which he stalks his prey (a cheetah, for example). It may not have eaten for several days, but it will still wait patiently for the appropriate moment to attack.

Its nourishment depends on its skill as a hunter, so it is only logical that it would be quite proficient at this task.

One aspect of its skill (an aspect that is easy to overlook) is patience. It knows, innately or by experience, that if it allows a nagging belly to impair its judgment, it will only have to wait longer for its next meal.

So, the cheetah calmly waits while collecting data that will shape its attack plan. Which gazelle will be the easiest victim? Which gazelle will stray into range first?

When the appropriate moment arrives, the cheetah unhesitatingly launches its attack, mercilessly closing on its target with single-minded determination.

There is no anger and no emotion in the cheetah. It simply tears its victim down in the most efficient manner possible, not stopping until the struggle is over.

This is the epitome of killer instinct. There is a vast wealth of knowledge to be gained from studying predatory animals.

If you compare the Jeet Kune Do game plan with that of the cheetah, you will find many similarities. In the embryonic stages of a street fight, we make our preliminary analysis.

This will include any observations about our adversary's structure (boxer, karate man, wrestler, etc.). Our preliminary analysis must be as accurate as possible, because tactical choices will be made from this data. It cannot be tainted by too much emotion.

Just as the cheetah looks for the weakest gazelle, we look for any apparent weakness in our opponent's defense.

It would not be particularly wise for the cheetah to hunt the strongest, fastest gazelle. Nor would it make sense for us to try to outbox a stronger, faster boxer.

In our case, we don't stand around waiting for an opportunity, but try to create one by moving and probing.

Through this process we can get the opponent to reveal much more about himself than he would probably like, and possibly even make a mistake. When the time is right, we enter, straight blast, and finish our opponent with an unrelenting barrage of headbutts, knees and elbows.

This is the point of no return. We must assume that our survival depends upon the success of this technique and our emotional intensity must reflect this belief.

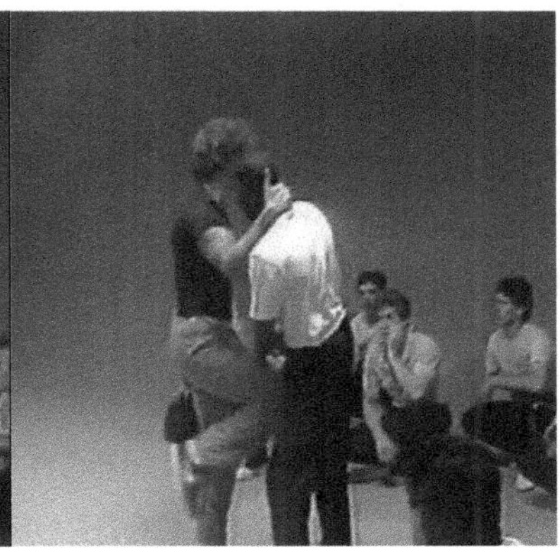

To reach the full potential of our killer instinct, we must control our emotional make-up. We have to go from a cold, unfeeling machine to a raging grizzly bear and back again in a second if the situation calls for it.

In kicking and punching range, we must be that machine, free from any emotional tension or anxiety. We dispassionately view the situation and react to it as if it were a blatantly obvious course of action.

Once we enter into trapping range, we must become a wild animal, oblivious to pain or reason. If the fight goes to the ground, we must kick back into machine mode so we can effectively make the correct tactical decisions.

There is a common misconception that someone who angers easily or "blows his top" regularly has a lot of "killer instinct." Not true.

This is simply a person who is being led around by his emotions. To me it's like a little kid having a temper tantrum!

Legendary basketball coach Phil Jackson, in his book Sacred Hoops, talks about emotional control...

"It was no coincidence that the players had a hard time staying focused against Detroit.

The Pistons' primary objective was to throw us off our game by raising the level of violence on the floor... I realized that anger was the Bulls' real enemy, not the Detroit Pistons."

Anger clouds the judgment and hinders concentration.

By teaching his players to stay composed emotionally in the face of a physical confrontation, Jackson ensured that attempts to rattle the Bulls with violent shoving, elbowing or punching failed to produce the desired results.

This level of control is not easy to reach. It can only be achieved if we are aware of the changes going on inside ourselves. As the biofeedback axiom goes, control follows awareness.

So, the question is, if control follows awareness, how do we reach this awareness?

First, we must see killer instinct in a light unobscured by any moralistic or idealistic shade.

We need to realize it is not something to be feared, something to be ashamed of, or something to be carefully hidden away within the deepest part of our minds.

Killer instinct is present in each and every one of us. The dilemma, then, becomes what to do with it.

In some people, it needs to be tamed or suppressed to a degree. Others need to bring it out more. To turn it on or off at will is an incredibly valuable asset, which can only be achieved by proper training and self-knowledge.

Awareness is being cognizant of the mental, spiritual, emotional and physiological ramification of the moment.

Awareness is being in tune with your surroundings, sensing your effect on them as well as their effect on you.

For example, if someone cuts you off in traffic and you experience an overwhelming urge to separate this person's head from his body, you don't instantly clamp down and suppress this urge while berating yourself for your Neanderthal behavior.

You simply acknowledge what you are feeling at the moment, what caused you to feel this way, and how you can use this knowledge to your benefit should a real situation arise.

Awareness can be cultivated in many ways. Specifically, right now, we are only concerned with awareness in one's self, but the attributes necessary for street awareness can certainly be useful here.

However, the catch is that we are dealing with something intrinsically more difficult. We come from a culture of distraction. Television, radio, video games, phones, and endless juicy tabloids serve to distract us from dealing with our seemingly mundane lives.

By divorcing ourselves from reality, if only for a moment, we lose touch with the one thing that determines our potential for accomplishment - ourselves.

How many hours have you spent by yourself, free from any sort of distraction - even hunting or backpacking? I mean time spent walking or sitting, listening only to your body. This is no easy task.

Sitting quietly for 20 minutes a day for a week will tell you volumes about yourself. You will find all kinds of intense emotions surfacing for no apparent reason. Your mind will concoct very persuasive arguments against this course of action.

This will not be a pleasant experience. Now, I am not espousing any religious and/or spiritual doctrines for this practice.

This is simply an exercise to cultivate awareness, because if you can't listen to your body sitting still, you aren't going to hear a thing when Gunnery Sergeant Pat Bagley is drilling uppercuts into your ribs!

Let's say you heeded my advice and now have a working level of awareness. Here's where we get to work on the control aspect. (This is actually the easier part.)

Now that you are aware of the changes going on in your body, you should simply try to effect gradual control over these changes. The more acute your awareness, the more successful your attempts will be.

Any situation that causes your blood to boil or your heart to beat a little faster is an opportunity for training. It could be a fight with your mate, a particularly condescending teller at the bank or a check that was supposed to be in the mail. Anything that gets you going is fair game.

Instead of flying off the handle, causing considerable damage to your home and furnishings, or suppressing the powerful emotions at play (thereby causing you an ulcer), take a few deep breaths and acknowledge what's happening in your body.

You may still be angry, but now it is a controlled anger, which provides eminently usable energy.

Make no mistake: Anybody can throw a temper tantrum. Losing your cool is not a sign of strength, but lack of control. A lot of this may seem obscure, but it really isn't.

Think of any great sports figure and pay attention to how he thrives under pressure. He feels the emotions as strongly as the next man, but he knows how to channel and not be overwhelmed by them.

As fighters, we must always be aware of our actions. Not only for the safety of others, but more because we can then act appropriately, decisively, and ruthlessly when the need arises to defend our loved ones or ourselves.

The killer instinct is not a sledgehammer but a scalpel that must be continually honed. Killer instinct will allow us to prevail in an ear-biting, eye-gouging street fight.

It is the savvy that clues us into our adversary's weakness. It is the ruthlessness that drives you to mercilessly capitalize on that weakness. It is the impetus that turns your training into fighting.

This topic should not be taken lightly. If you intend to be a fighter, you should implement killer instinct development into your training.

The physical logistics of integrating these concepts into your training is up to you, but they must be grounded in these immutable principles. In a crisis, you will not rise to your expectations, but fall to your level of training. Don't let ignorance of killer instinct be your downfall.

Chapter 5: The Single Most Devastating Technique

I have been asked many times, “If you had to teach a student only ONE 'technique' (the straight lead, the hook kick, etc.) what would that 'technique' be?”

Answer: "The Eyes Have It." I would teach he or she to attack any adversary or assailant's eyes with the human body's most natural and most efficient strike.

This is a lighting fast backhand strike to the perpetrator's eyes. The eye is the only organ on the body that directly touches the brain and we simply refer to the eyeball as the “off button.”

This means that when you hit one eye it affects both and usually will bring a sudden and vicious end to any altercation.

To validate this point, one only needs to do the following:

Identify your weapon. Do this by taking the back of the hand and it's first 2 knuckles on all of your fingers.

Turn your hand so that you can see your palm and then strike the palm of your other hand with this tool. It is kind of a 'high-five' type of motion only using the back of the hand.

It follows a very natural line of attack and resembles the traditional Karate back-fist technique.

Practice by having someone hold a focus pad while the other person hits a small round target the size of a quarter on the pad. This will teach accuracy and correct placement of this all-around fight-ender.

To get an idea of just how potent this one weapon might be in any altercation, try it on yourself.

No, please do not send yourself to the emergency room. Just take the back of your hand using the aforementioned knuckles and lightly tap your own eye.

Then gradually increase the impact until you get the idea of just how stunning and vicious this strike can be.

A good MD friend of mine told me that this strike is, structurally, the fastest strike on the human body.

In a grabbing, holding, wrestling or any position that does not allow the freedom of motion to use this tool then we would attack with the Kina Mutay ' eye gouge.

One simply grabs the assailant's neck or head and applies either an eye gouge or eye rake. If you have long finger nails then the raking attack has its advantages.

If your nails are short, then the gouge or sinking the fingers into the eye-socket works well. Ok, that's it. Pretty simple and easy to learn.

Almost immediately functional and a very potent weapon to use in any self-defense situation.

Chapter 6: Interview with Paul Vunak

PFS: What was your first art?

PV: Tae Kwon Do... I started at age 9 and studied for four years.

PFS: Who was your instructor?

PV: Actually, there were four instructors that ran the school. They were called the Yi Brothers - I believe their names were Yung Pok, Yung Kuk, Yung Ho, and Yung Chuen.

PFS: Why did you leave the Yi Brothers?

PV: After I finally got a black belt I decided to move on. I felt my kicking techniques were OK, however, I lacked good hands.

PFS: What was your next school?

PV: Tiger-Crane Kenpo Karate... it was an offshoot of BKF (Black Karate Federation). A gentleman by the name of Al Fleming was my instructor.

PFS: How long did you study there?

PV: For roughly three years.

PFS: Why did you leave?

PV: Well, I ended up doing most of the teaching there and soon discovered that our school had turned into a childcare center. I had about 25-30 adults (mostly in their late twenties) and over 50 kids.

My emphasis was on fighting and not on running a business, so I got the brainy idea to close down the kids' class. Three months later, our school closed down.

PFS: Why is it that you were more interested in fighting than business?

PV: I grew up that way... I witnessed a lot of fighting starting from a very young age. I was living in the worst part of Long Beach, California. In my high school (Poly High), being Caucasian meant you were the minority.

Not to mention growing up in an extremely emotional household with a Yugoslavian father and a Sicilian mother!

PFS: Where did you go after the BKF school?

PV: It was November 22, 1976 when I was first introduced to Dan Inosanto and the Filipino Kali Academy.

PFS: What was that like?

PV: I remember there were some dividers separating the classes. Most people don't know, but the old Kali Academy used to teach Kenpo Karate as well as Jeet Kune Do and Kali.

I remember showing up on a Saturday afternoon during which there were no formal classes, just free workout time. I decided to spar with someone to confirm that this was indeed the school for me.

PFS: What was the result of this encounter?

PV: I picked the biggest, most serious-looking guy in the school and asked him if he would spar with me.

My adrenaline was pumping and I was bent on taking this guy out. I also remember hitting this guy with a backfist... that's the last thing I remember!

When I woke up, there was a bunch of guys staring down at me, and I remember my first words were, "Sign me up!"

PFS: Did you ever meet up with this guy again?

PV: (laughing) Yeah, we became friends and trained very hard together. His name was Torrance Mathis.

I remember after he kicked my ass all over the gym, I had car trouble and he drove me home. I sat on my bed staring at a wall full of trophies and certificates until, in tears, I ripped every certificate off my wall.

I vividly remember my Mom walking in during my adolescent emotional outburst and asking what happened to my face. When I told her she said, “So I guess those two black belts and a quarter will get you a cup of coffee.”

PFS: So where did you go from there?

PV: After about three years at the Kali Academy, I started teaching there.

PFS: What year are we in right now?

PV: I was 19, so it must have been around late '79.

PFS: What were your days like teaching at the Kali Academy?

PV: Eventually I ended up teaching several classes daily. I opened the doors at 4:00 every afternoon, and our last class ended at 10:00 PM. A handful of us would stay every night until 2:00 AM talking to Dan.

PFS: So, you spent 8-10 hours a day there, 7 days a week?

PV: No, we were closed on Sundays.

PFS: Why the hectic schedule?

PV: Well, I was basically supporting myself from age 17 on through teaching.

During the time I was training and teaching at the Kali Academy I also had a Savate school with Daniel Duby from 1980-1984. [Ed. note: This was the first Savate school inthe United States.]

I've never had a real J.O.B. Actually, that's not true... I worked at Kentucky Fried Chicken for 3.5 days. I was the Extra Crispy Man!

PFS: How long did you keep up this training pace?

PV: Basically, until the Kali Academy closed down... so, from 1976 - 1984. I then continued to study with Dan at Culver City for the next two years. That's when I formed my own organization, Progressive Fighting Systems. However, I never stopped being Dan's student.

PFS: How did you go about setting up the organization?

PV: During the years I spent teaching under Dan, my private clientele had grown rather large. A lot of times, students would ask Dan for private instruction in certain specific areas, then he would direct them to the most appropriate instructors.

For example, if someone wanted stick fighting, Dan would send him to Ted Lucay. For boxing, he would usually guide them to Richard Bustillo. For people interested in raw street fighting, Dan would send them my way.

Consequently, PFS is comprised of people all over the world with the same bent - the pursuit of pure fighting and self-defense.

PFS: How many people belong to the organization?

PV: We have over 300 instructors and over 4,000 students worldwide.

PFS: Do you own all 300 schools?

PV: No, I didn't learn anything from KFC, this is not a franchise! PFS is an organization of all friends, in which I get to be more of a guide than a boss. We really only have two basic goals:

1) Undying loyalty to Dan Inosanto.

2) To help keep Kali and Jeet Kune Do alive and growing in an ethical and responsible way.

PFS: Could you explain your ranking system?

PV: To understand our ranking system, you first need to understand the methodology of learning Jeet Kune Do.

It has everything to do with the process, and little to do with the product! In other words, one becomes proficient in JKD through the process of self-discovery... and self-discovery is fueled by the process of teaching.

This mentality started when Bruce Lee first came to America; he had his mother art of

Wing Chun, but after discovering certain limitations he would essentially experiment on his students by teaching them.

This gave him people to train with - absolutely crucial for him to develop! Dan Inosanto is the main link between us and Bruce's principles and concepts. After Bruce passed away, Dan was left with the mantle of "Jeet Kune Do" on his shoulders.

In order for him to continue the growth of the art, he opened up the Filipino Kali Academy. This school was like no other, we were basically a giant garage full of hard-core students.

People would come from all over the world to view Bruce's art... professional boxers, Thai boxers, world-class Karate and Gung-fu men, and about every other style you can imagine. We had two words for anyone who came with a negative attitude: "Glove up!"

I remember our school had a "bad rap." People would say, "They aren't martial artists, they're just interested in fighting." The floors had seen so much blood, we finally gave up and painted them red!

The Kali Academy was the laboratory in which the art that we learn now was developed. When the Academy closed and I started PFS, I needed bodies to teach, in order for me to personally continue growing.

The only way I know how to teach is to get my students to a particular level and then allow them to take the concepts and principles and teach students of their own.

By the process of teaching Jeet Kune Do Concepts, my students are accelerating their personal growth tenfold.

After roughly ten hours of very intense one-on-one training with me, I usually award an apprentice instructorship.

This does not mean that these individuals are qualified Jeet Kune Do instructors! It simply means one has our blessing to teach what he or she knows and to grow from the experience. (Hence the term "apprentice.")

After roughly fifty hours of private instruction with me (or 2-5 years of training in a group setting, and depending on skill and other factors), an apprentice will receive the first official rank of instructorship, Phase One Instructor.

At this point, after several years of dedication to learning, to Dan Inosanto and to PFS, a Full instructorship is awarded.

All of my full instructors must not only have the physical side of the art groomed well, but the mental and emotional sides as well. Full instructors can make their own apprentice instructors.

Finally, we have the rank of Senior Instructor. All of our Senior Instructors have been around for ten years or more. They must exhibit not only all the attributes of the full instructors, but also have a solid belief system.

Our Senior instructors have evolved to the point where they are exploring the spiritual side of the art. It takes absolute determination and persistence to achieve this level, the highest attainable in PFS.

Seniors can make apprentice and Phase One instructors.

PFS: When did you start your Jiu Jitsu training?

PV: June of '88 was when I had my first taste of Jiu Jitsu. I was studying with Rorion (Gracie) in his garage.

PFS: What do you remember most about training with the Gracies?

PV: I guess it would be that wonderful feeling of training your whole life standing up and then having someone completely play with you on the ground.

Not to sound like a fanatic or anything, but I was reborn! I consider myself to this day, after ten years, still a baby on the ground. I get to be a student for the rest of my life.

PFS: Which of the Gracies did you train with besides Rorion?

PV: Besides about a year and a half with him, I worked with Royce for about the same amount of time, Royler for about 6 months, and Rickson for about three years.

PFS: Why did you train with all four of the Gracies?

PV: They all have a different "feel" and perception of how things are done.

PFS: Not to play favorites, but did you "connect" with any particular brother in a special way?

PV: Well, they're all incredible ground fighters, but anyone who has ever rolled around for even five minutes with Rickson will tell you that he's from another planet!

Besides an intense appreciation for the years I had with him, I have no words to describe his skill level.

There are certain athletes who defy description... Bruce Lee, Michael Jordan, Wayne Gretzky, Rickson Gracie... I guess God was in a good mood when he was dishing out attributes for these guys! (Laughs.)

PFS: Were other JKD practitioners studying Jiu Jitsu also?

PV: Very, very few. I think that for most people who have dedicated years to the martial arts and are already teachers, it is too difficult to put on a Gi, strap on a white belt, and start all over as a student.

PFS: What was your next evolutionary phase?

PV: Well, I got absolutely fanatical about Jiu Jitsu... I spread the word about Gracie Jiu Jitsu from South Dakota to South Africa.

No one outside of Brazil had really even heard of the Gracies back then, so I integrated the training into all of my schools worldwide. Later the Gracies opened up a school and then came the UFC.

Now they're a household name. I'm glad and honored that I got to train with them back when they were more accessible.

PFS: When did you start teaching the Navy SEALs?

PV: They initially approached me in late '88.

PFS: Why did they come to you?

PV: I have no idea. I was originally approached by a gentleman named Monty Trezise, who interviewed me extensively and then directed me to Frank Gucci.

After an eye-to-eye meeting, Frank became very enthusiastic and spearheaded my relocation to Virginia.

PFS: Which teams did you work with?

PV: Mainly Team 6; however, I eventually got around to most of the teams in one capacity or another. We did most of the training on base; however, a few times I would work with teams preparing for more covert operations and we would train off base in a banquet room at a nearby hotel.

PFS: How long did you stay in Virginia?

PV: For a very long three years.

PFS: Why do you say "very long?"

PV: Because I really didn't like living in Virginia. All we ever did was train all day, and go to biker bars and drink beer and fight every night.

PFS: Training Navy SEALs and kicking butt sounds like a martial artist's dream!

PV: It's very easy to romanticize things like that, but in actuality there's nothing dreamy about waking up in jail with crusted blood, swollen knuckles, and dry heaves.

PFS: So how did you end up back in California?

PV: I actually had about six months left on my contract with the military, but I negotiated with the powers-that-be to delegate the rest of the teaching to three people.

These guys had been my most persistent, talented, and dedicated students. They were Pat Bagley, Pat Tray, and Frank Gucci. I certified them as Full Instructors to carry on my art with my blessing.

Thus, I was able to move back home to California. Now I only go back occasionally when my services are requested for a special operation.

Chapter 7: Bruce Lee, Dan Lee Interview

This is a transcript of a taped interview. The tape begins midway through a sentence spoken by Bruce Lee, who is describing how unprepared for real combat the Chinese martial artists were that he witnessed during a recent tournament in Hong Kong...

- Bruce Lee is in bold,

- Dan Lee is not.

Bruce Lee: ... You saw the Tai Chi self-defense; you saw all the self-defense in there. It's all posturing.

Well, Dan, Dan, Dan, I mean I hate to tell you this; if you were there with... plus the foreign friends sitting next to us watching the Goks and Bai Choys - Jesus, you would be so embarrassed!

Dan Lee: Yeah, it's like a free-brawl

Bruce Lee: It's not even a fee-brawl. You see a free-brawl, at least, I mean, that's Joe Frazier! I mean a man who is capable of using his tools. And who is very determined in his savage, relentless, attack. Whereas those sons of bitches are cowards.

I mean, turning their heads [away from their opponent while they are] swinging

their punch, and, after the second rough, they're out of breath. I mean, they're really pathetic looking, I mean, very, very, amateurish.

I mean even a boxer, when they concentrate on [just using their] two hands - disregard how amateurish they are - they do their thing!

Dan Lee: That's right; they're in a war.

Bruce Lee: Whereas [when] those guys go out there, they haven't decided what the hell they're gonna use!

I mean, before they [make] contact with each other, they do all the fancy stance and all the fancy movement but, the minute they [make] contact, they don't know what the hell they're going to do! I mean that's it.

They miss and they fall on their asses, and they clutch and hold and wrestle, and, I mean, the whole Hong Kong, they call it "little kids fighting."

That's their interpretation - even in Hong Kong! I mean can you imagine that? I mean even those guys see it that way, so

what do you think the appreciation of people over here [would be]? Well, none - period. So, what I'm hoping to do in film is to be just that, man. To raise the level ...

Dan Lee: You have a real mission there.

Bruce Lee: Yeah, really. It not only will raise the level but you have to upgrade [the level of martial art over there]to gain respect from the Western world.

That's what I hope to do, man! Because like here, I mean the reason I'm coming back is Warner Bros. wants me to do a television series but I don't think I'll do it now.

I'm going to concentrate on Hong Kong and do it. And actually, I might be able to expand it to here like the Italian pictures such as A Fistful of Dollars and things like that - if the quality can be uplifted.

And that's what I'm... you know, more and more simple to me [laughs] as a human being. And more and more I search myself and the more and more the questions are more and more listed and

more and more I see clearly. It's really the simplicity.

It is. It really is, man. What it is, is that what man has to get over is the consciousness. The consciousness of himself.

Dan Lee: I always remember you saying "you have to sharpen your tools." That's it too; if your tools are working properly, then you can use them.

Bruce Lee: That's it, you see? Here it is: if you can move with your tools from any angle, then you can adapt to whatever the object is in front of you.

And the clumsier, the more limited the object, the easier for you to potshot it. [laughs] That's what it amounts to!

Really what it is, is that it utilizes the body to come to some sort of a realization in this regard as to whatever your pursuit might be.

In my case, the pursuit of becoming moment to moment, whatever that thing is. And constantly questioning myself; "What is this, Bruce?" "Is it true or is it not true?"

"Do you really mean it or not mean it" Once when I've found that out, that's it. I mean, like my coming back to refuse the television series is one of the major decisions.

Dan Lee: You've actually reached the point; where you've become quite philosophical. You see the ultimate goal.

Bruce Lee: Well, let me say this, I haven't as yet been able to control my anger. I mean, violent anger. Well, this comes with age [laughs].

Well, not only that, but I mean if I would only take the time to just stop for a few minutes I would be able to control it - but unfortunately, I mean, like, let's say if Lo Tai-Chuen were man enough - instead of going to the newspaper - to walk up to me and slap me - that's the end of him!

I mean, [laughs] I have yet been able to "turn the other cheek," man.

Dan Lee: Well in fact I think the fact that now unlike ten years ago when you would have said "okay, Lo Tai-Chuen, pick the time!"

Bruce Lee: "Pick the time?" I wouldn't - "pick the time?" - I wouldn't even say anything! I would just show up right in front of his door waiting for him!

That's all there is to it. I mean, I have yet refused one challenge ever since I was in the United States - all these B.S. artists, all of them. They mention it. I just accept it.

I mean, you know the first question I ask myself is this: "Do I have any fear or any doubt about this man?" - I don't. "Do I know what his intention is?" - Yes, I do.

"So what the hell you gonna do about it?" - Nothin! [laughs] That's it! I mean it takes a hell of a lot for me not to do anything than to do something.

Dan Lee: The fact that you made this decision actually [reveals]a process of maturity.

Bruce Lee: That's right [catches himself] - not "maturity - there is no such word as "maturity." Rather: "matur-ing."

Dan Lee: "Matur-ing?"

Bruce Lee: Damn right, man.

Dan Lee: As in constantly striving?

Bruce Lee: Yes, because when there is a maturity, there is a conclusion and a cessation, man. That's the end. That's when the coffin is closed.

I mean, you might be deteriorating physically in the long process of aging but, man, in your daily discovery - it's still the very same every day.

Dan Lee: I think you're actually getting to the point of- you remember the two "Chinese Scrolls: Yee Mo Faat, Wai Yao Fatt?"

Bruce Lee: Yee Mo Faat, Wai Yao Fatt, Yee Mo Haan, Wai Yai Hann." You're reaching these points.

Approaching these points. Yeah, that's the most important thing, man. Because when there is a "Way," man, therein lies the limitation. And when there is a circumference, it traps. And if it traps, it rottens. And if it rottens, it is lifeless.

Dan Lee: That's right. Well, whatever you've said has made a great impact in my training, in my thinking in martial art as a whole.

I mean it seems like once you talk to you and work on this, you never ever go back to what you've been doing; Kempa or whatever it is; you reach another level of understanding and you looking back.

Bruce Lee: Well, because man [the species] is constantly growing. And when he is bound by a set pattern of ideas or "Way" of doing things, that's when he stops growing.

Dan Lee: Yeah, very much so.

Bruce Lee: [laughs] Yeah, well, I'm lucky. That's about it.

Dan Lee: Well actually you have influenced many people in terms of freedom from their original boundaries.

Bruce Lee: Well, I hope so.

Dan Lee: Danny [Inosanto] was just excited all over yesterday! He was really turned on. Yeah, he was at my house the night before.

So, he doesn't want us to do any more heavy bag; he wants us to just actually [use the] instep a little bit. We just had three people [training] yesterday. That's all he's going to teach within our little group.

Bruce Lee: Yes, because when you use your leg it is much better to use it to kick at the foam pad or something like that. Watch out with the side kick on air kicking too much because it's bad for the knee joint.

Dan Lee: The knee joint is dangerous, huh?

Bruce Lee: Well, I mean, if you snap it too much without resistance at the end, you know? Just think about economical movement.

Dan Lee: Did you know that there is a kickboxing association right on Hollywood Boulevard? I've yet to go see it.

Bruce Lee: They have kickboxing? You have seen kickboxing? I saw it in Thailand, personally. The bantamweight champion, in fact, was one of the stuntmen in our film. Well, the problem with them is that they are the "John L. Sullivans" of the feet. I mean, no finesse.

Dan Lee: I imagine that if they manage to step in and rap you on the rear of your thigh - that's what usually causes their opponents to completely give up; they just rap them into it.

Bruce Lee: Well, not all of them do that, I mean they can do that [to you] if you are stationary, but not when you are constantly moving- I mean, man!

The Japanese martial artists have incorporated the sweeping kick under the Thai fighter's high [hook] kick - you can really see the Thailand people when they reach - their foot is in the air and then [they] try to kick.

And the moment they kick the Japanese drop and move in and sweep their foot away or make a Judo throw and the Thai is having trouble just maintaining balance because the kick is too high. And too obvious!

That's the whole deal, you see. There is no subtleness, no economy.

That's why... No subtleness - and no broken rhythm either! You can see it coming! That's it - "John L. Sullivan!" That's why 80 percent of their knockouts are by hand.

Dan Lee: Then why would this guy who owns the kickboxing school be making all kinds of boasts?

Bruce Lee: Oh man, you just put him in the ring [with a western boxer], man, the boxer would just beat the hell out of him. So, that goes to show you.

END OF INTERVIEW

Chapter 8:
5 Secrets to Surviving an Assault

1. Know When You're in A Fight.

Often, people lose a fight because they don't realize they are in one until it is too late! Establish your personal zones and limits of personal security.

Pre-determine decisions based upon the violation of those zones. You should already have determined what you will do if you discover someone in your house at night.

You should know how close you will let someone get to you that may be brandishing an edged weapon. You should know when a verbal confrontation is escalating to a high level what your choice will be and how you will act.

You should have a plan if strangers approach your car in a parking lot or at a stoplight. These are not decisions you want to ponder in the stunned reality of the moment. Pre-determine your choices and your actions.

2. Awareness and Avoidance.

Awareness and Avoidance are the two common attributes that are emphasized more than any other tactic, technique or device!

Your awareness of your surroundings, the people, the location, the exits, the potential improvised weapons, obstructions, cover, concealment and the like will give you the edge in any situation. This level of awareness will often help you to avoid physical assaults and confrontations.

Small choices in everyday life can make a big difference in avoiding, escaping or surviving a physical assault. Choices like sitting in a restaurant with your back to the wall so you can see anyone and everyone approaching you.

Leaving enough space between you and the car in front of you to avoid being boxed in and car jacked. Driving in the right-hand lane to avoid a carjacker from approaching your driver side window.

3. Always Strike First.

This may seem contrary to what you learned in grade school. If you want to win a fight, STRIKE FIRST! If you don't, you will be reacting rather than acting.

In short, 99.9% of the time you will lose. Warning: DO NOT DEPEND UPON ONE TECHNIQUE OR PUNCH TO END THE CONFLICT!

We all like to believe that like John Wayne or Dirty Harry, we have this one haymaker punch that will knock anyone's lights out. You don't! Few people do. If you did, you'd still be a fool to rely upon it.

Continue your attack on your attacker until you have undoubtedly and unquestionably stopped the threat. Anything short is a gamble with your own wellbeing.

Learn a small stable of target points. Knees strikes, foot stomps, one knuckle floating rib shots, throat crushes, eye jabs, head butts... whatever.

4. Create your personal "First & Best" move arsenal.

Most great fighters have a stable or arsenal of personal favorite moves. It's imperative that you learn a few reliable and devastating moves to pull out when you need them most.

These moves should be easy to learn and master and not rely upon a high degree of athleticism. Simple and pragmatic techniques like foot stomps, head butts, eye gouges, groin kicks can be utilized in almost any location, in any weather, wearing just about any clothes.

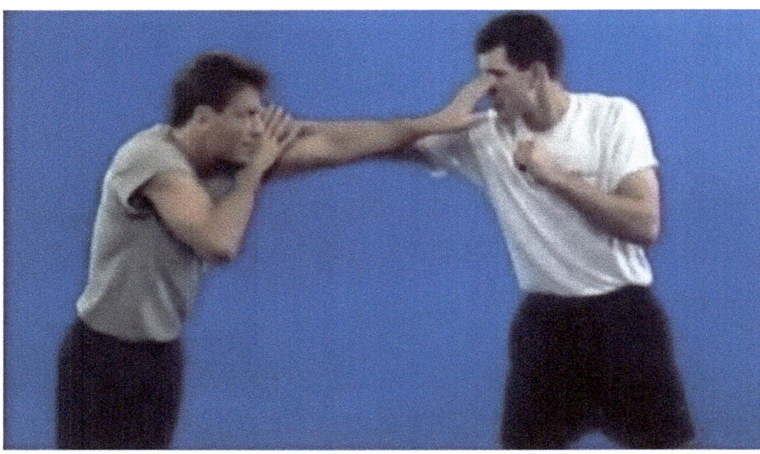

Fancy disarms and joint locks are cool and can work if you practice them. But you'll serve yourself well to start with choices that involve gross natural motor skills.

That will make them reliable. Learn the sensitive and vulnerable targets of the body and attack, attack, attack with a flurry of your personal "First and Best" moves.

5. Remember, there are NO RULES!

You must develop, use and display a complete and total disregard for your opponent's wellbeing.

You must choose to survive the assault and use whatever force is necessary to stop the threat. Gentlemen don't assault people.

Take those honor bound gentlemanly civil society rules about nasty tactics such as groin shots, eye gouges, lip, nose and ear tearing, flesh biting etc., and throw them out the window. You're there to win.

The prize of the fight may be... your LIFE!

Chapter 9: Women's Self-Defense: Escape to Gain Safety

The time an individual spends in the martial arts (both frequency and duration) depends on his or her motivation.

While some find it enough to take a few classes or a seminar, others dedicate their lifetimes to the "way." I frequently encounter people with varied reasons for participation in the arts.

This chapter is not geared toward the female martial artist, but rather toward women who may have taken a weekend self-defense or a "rape prevention" course, and left either with a false sense of security or feeling more confusion than confidence.

Many women never intend to dedicate more than the minimum amount of time it takes for them to feel more confident in an attack situation.

Questioning them illustrates the overwhelming worry that the majority of women share: "I'm afraid if it were real, I would just freeze up and forget everything!" The words "forget" and "everything" imply they think they have a lot to remember.

Unfortunately, most instructors rarely adapt their art to the average woman. Catering to these students is essential and requires consideration of the following points:

1. Most men often begin martial arts training with the preconceived notion that they will soon be kicking butt and taking names. A woman, however, sees a radically different and more frightening picture.

Her mind is on the serious realities of an attack/rape. Others like her are being assaulted every day. Knowing this causes her to develop a legitimate worry (not convoluted by the male ego or delusions of grandeur fostered by Billy Jack movies).

2. Women have a different morphology, generally speaking, from men. And so, they must learn different techniques and principles, which emphasize different qualities (attributes) and use different training methods than the average male martial artist.

3. Finally, most women simply don't put in the same fight time in a self-defense class that a man might in the dojo. He can get away with learning technique upon technique, kata upon kata, addicted to the black belt "carrot" being dangled in front of him.

For these reasons, women who want self-defense will find that the traditional arts' myriad of techniques, usually better suited for a tournament fight than a street attack, simply don't constitute a viable self-defense program.

The mentality of "if he does this, then you do that" is ineffective because there are too many things "he" can do!

If a specific technique is taught for each possible scenario, the very fear most women express may well come true - they will freeze up and forget everything.

Jeet Kune Do encompasses aspects that perfectly translate into an effective self-defense approach for women.

Two major JKD concepts central to women's self-defense are adaptability and simplicity. Any techniques taught as part of a self-defense program have to be simple; that is, they should be easy to learn, easy to do, and easy to remember.

All techniques should also be adaptable. In other words, a technique should work in a variety of situations against a variety of attacks. I developed a program specifically for women and non-martial artists, which addresses these specific needs.

This program is called "Escape to Gain Safety." It decreases the fear of forgetting a multitude of techniques, while effectively dealing with most attack scenarios.

The way in which a woman is attacked is not of paramount importance in the Escape to Gain Safety program. Rather, the program emphasizes Bruce Lee's concept of attacking the closest target with the longest weapon.

A man assaulting a woman rarely (if ever) begins in a stance, jabbing or kicking. Close-quarter scenarios (grabs, pulls, or holds) make up a large part (at least 85 percent) of the attacks being considered.

Now that the woman's attention is placed on striking a target instead of remembering a technique for each possible situation (there could be an infinite number of these), where to hit becomes the all-important question.

Virtually every attack exposes effective targets for a solid strike. There are only four targets to be concerned with, one or more of which will always be available: The eyes, throat, groin and shins. These are vulnerable areas on the body, regardless of size, strength, or physical conditioning.

Obviously, the best defense is common sense and preventative steps such as avoiding high-risk areas whenever possible. Try to steer clear of alleyways, dark streets and parking lots at night or when alone.

Proper psychology can also be very important if avoidance fails, but when it comes down to it, what to say to an assailant can be just as difficult to remember as what to do to him.

So, should an attack become physical, a woman's strategy should be simple as well. Too often, women are taught sequences of several follow-up blows. Although it might look good in the gym, this is not recommended.

Once the first effective blow is delivered and the attacker is momentarily distracted or stunned, scream and run like hell!

When an attacker gets his eyes or throat jabbed, his groin hit, or his shin smashed, it is unlikely he will have quite the same intent to chase her down the street for another try! The desired outcome is to survive, not overcome an attacker.

Now let's go back to the original (and legitimate) worry plaguing most women: Forgetting the techniques.

All a woman has to remember is striking, grabbing, or biting one of the four targets. Those targets fit into a convenient acronym:

Escape	**To**	**Gain**	**Safety**
y	**h**	**r**	**h**
e	**r**	**o**	**i**
s	**o**	**i**	**n**
	a	**n**	
	t		

Of course, locating and striking the targets effectively requires training.

No approach is guaranteed. However, I do guarantee this: One is less likely to forget everything one has learned if what one learns is less complicated.

This concept can benefit not only women, but also any martial artist or non-martial artist who wants to feel more confident about his or her own personal safety.

Say you are grabbed on either arm… boom, fire an eye jab right in the eye.

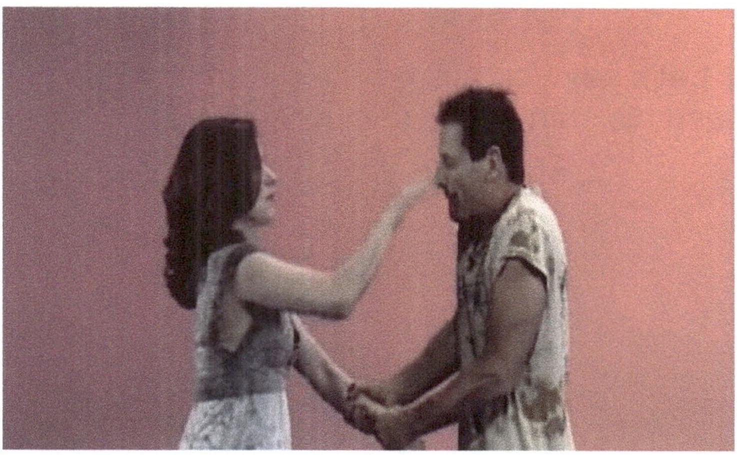

Say he grabs you with two hands, then you launch a knee to the groin.

Let’s say you are grabbed from behind. Smash his shin with a shin kick.

Escape To Gain Safety - Eyes, Throat, Groin and Shin.

Training Tip: Please remember, you don't have to think. We need something that is operable when the visceral response and the hypothalamus, and the pituitary gland are secreting, and your heart is pumping at full blast.

Chapter 10: Navy SEAL Quick Kills

You may find yourself in a situation where you need to a person's existence permanently. Our military units find themselves in these situations all the time.

So, what I'm about to teach you here, I wouldn't recommend doing it to someone that cut you off in traffic.

Training Tip: These are called Quick Kills and all I can say is that when you practice these, just stay away as far as you can when you train. Just for safety of course!

Quick Kill – Throat

From the Thai Clinch, you just got through doing a headbutt, now from this position, we will invoke our quick kill.

Training Tip: As you lift the chin, you want to expose the Adam's apple.

You can punch the throat pretty hard from here and believe it or not you can take it. But when you've exposed the Adam's apple, with just a little flick, this person's out of commission permanently.

So again, please be careful, when training that you don't come too close to the exposed Adam's apple. It is important when you do this that the person is looking up.

We're going to do this in slow motion. I always like to put my headbutts in, a little knee, a little thumb just to soften him up okay?

You want the guy to be looking straight up to the moon when the elbow goes across the Adam's apple.

That part is really important and of course for training, let's stay about 6 inches away.

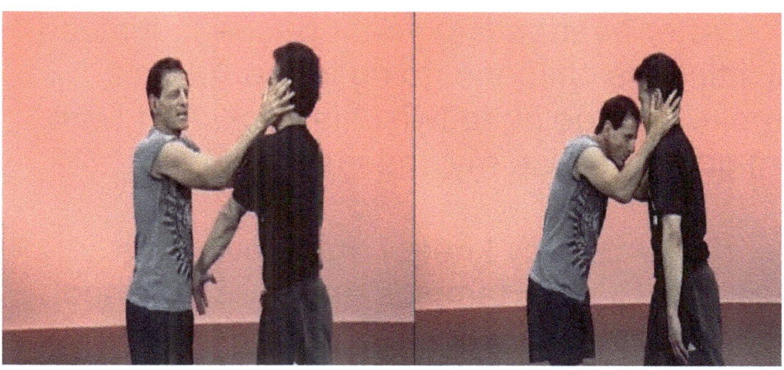

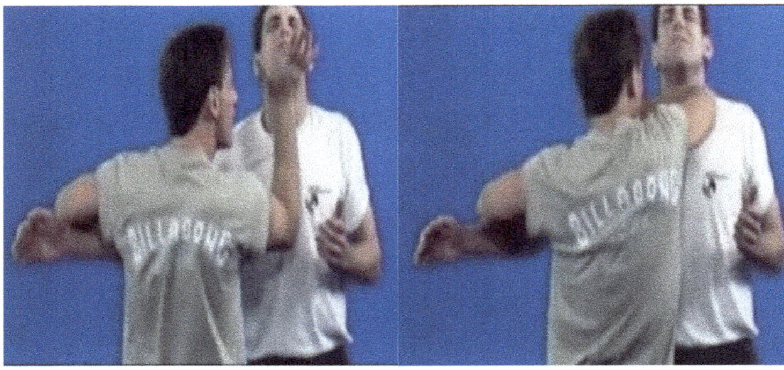

Like I said, an elbow to the Adam's apple will permanently disable any attacker.

Quick Kill - Temples

Our next quick kill also comes from the trapping range, from the Thai Clinch.

After headbutting your opponent, instead of lifting his chin and going to the Adam's Apple, I am going to twist his neck. As I twist, I'm going to raise my knee up.

As I raise my knee, I am shoving his head, so that his temples and my knee meet at the same time.

An elbow to exposed temple work well too. These techniques can cause the brain to swell and death to occur.

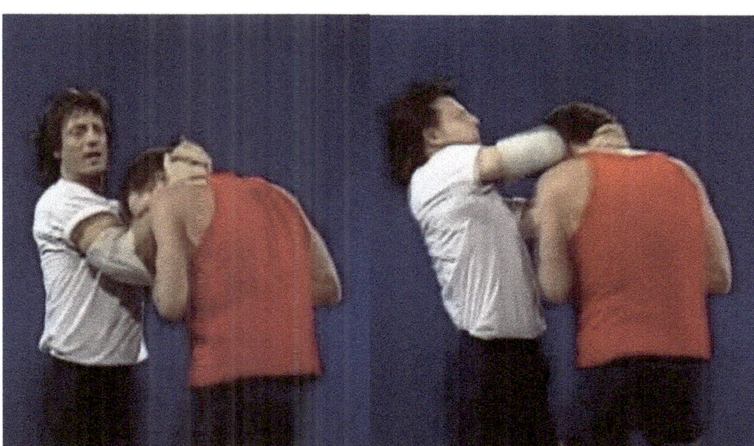

Training Tip: Be extremely careful when you do this, especially ascending of the knee, and keep your hand on his head for training. So, if you make a mistake, you're going to knee your own hand.

But in reality, you pull that hand away and drive that right up into the soft part of the brain. Once again, please, please, be careful.

Don't let the simplicity of these two moves fool you. They are simple for a reason. And, they will kill a man if you need to use them in a life-or-death fight.

Chapter 11: Filipino Art of Kina Mutay

As we look back on the history of the Philippines, we see much war and bloodshed. During many of the battles the Filipinos were forced to wage, they found themselves outnumbered and outgunned.

Imagine having to fight trained Samurai warriors using only farming equipment! Consequently, their ideology was to find a way to put them on equal footing with their adversaries.

They were forced to be incredibly innovative when dealing with the harsh reality of the times. When we use the word "circumvent" we are actually saying, "Find a way to cheat." In the world of weapons, the Filipinos developed an amazing way of "cheating."

Instead of blocking strikes, they would actually smash the opponent's weapon hand. By way of analogy, if the opponent was a snake and the weapon was the fang, this method was called “defanging the snake.”

While the rest of the world would go toe-to-toe weapons fighting, blocking strikes and trading blows, the Filipinos would simply and directly smash the hand.

They used the same ideology with when fighting with empty hands. Instead of blocking punches and kicks, they used nerve destructions against the incoming blows.

Instead of trading punches and kicks with their opponents, they would get inside and implement their knees, elbows, and headbutts.

Now that we are beginning to understand the central theme of the Filipino paradigm (David overcoming Goliath), let us delve into the world of grappling, and into the topic of this chapter Kina Mutay.

The term Kina Mutay literally means "the art of pinching and biting." In Jeet Kune Do we refer to it as "biting and eye gouging," because we prefer to pinch the eyeball. Many Filipino Escrimadores possessed an invaluable attribute that most people simply do not have: incredible grip strength.

This was a byproduct of wielding heavy sticks, swords and knives all day.

One of the most famous Filipino grandmasters, Floro Villabrille, could actually husk coconuts with his bare hands. This grip strength, combined with biting, is the Filipino way of "cheating" when it comes to grappling.

By no coincidence, Bruce Lee also possessed incredible grip strength. He used a lot of innovative equipment to develop that tendon strength in the fingers and forearms. When discussing eye gouging and biting, the first thing people say is, "Well, anyone can bite!"

This bland assertion is true - anyone can bite. But the difference between just plain biting and Kina Mutay is how to bite, where to bite, and when to bite. When a Kina Mutay practitioner bites you, it is with an uninterrupted bite.

This means he knows the exact places on the body to bite and with precise timing. He grabs you with his incredible grip strength and bites in areas that would take literally minutes to disengage.

There are over 140 areas on the human body that a Kina Mutay proponent can bite you and hang on for as long as he desires. While he is biting, he is implementing his knowledge of kinesiology along with the attributes of sensitivity and grip strength to hang on like a pit bull.

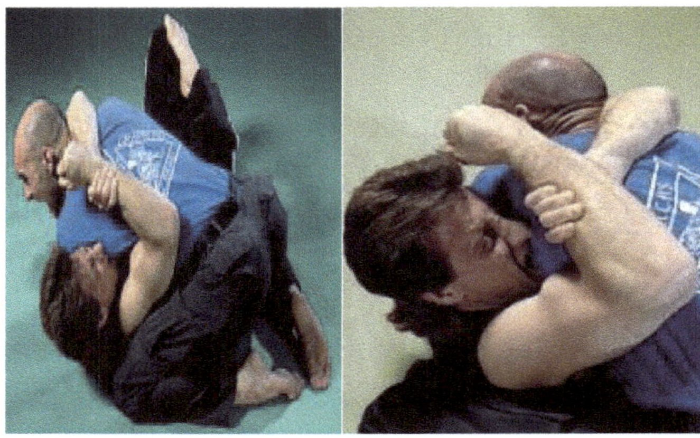

In the world of wrestling, Brazilian jiu-jitsu practitioners are clearly the kings. Their subtle body movements, ground sensitivity, knowledge of leverage, escapes and finishing moves are in a league of their own.

Combining the art of Brazilian jiu-jitsu with the Filipino art of Kina Mutay creates a hybrid grappling art that is perhaps the most formidable on the planet.

Kina Mutay allows us to circumvent the jiu-jitsu game. You could rely on Kina Mutay in a street fight against a bigger, stronger ground fighter to either beat him on the ground or create enough space to get back to your feet (even if your only goal is to run).

When there are no rules, weight classes or referees, "cheating" may be the only way to survive.

TRAINING METHODS OF KINA MUTAY

HOW TO BITE

In training in Kina Mutay we must first ascertain the essential principles and then work each individually. We will first focus on how to bite. A Kina Mutay practitioner is always cognizant of how much flesh is in his mouth.

The average person who doesn't know how to bite properly will try to use all his teeth and take too much "meat" in one bite.

Conversely, a Kina Mutay person will angle his face so the pressure is applied directly on the incisors. The actual motion of the bite is a repeated circular ripping of the flesh, which results in numerous smaller bites.

When applied cumulatively, unimaginable damage is inflicted.

The best way to practice this technique is to get a large piece of beef roast and put it inside a t-shirt. Next, get a timer and explode into your bite.

The goal is to tear through the entire piece of beef as quickly as possible. In the beginning of this drill, you will encounter several hurdles.

First, you will notice your teeth hydroplaning across the surface of the meat without actually penetrating. Varying the angle and pressure of the actual bite (using the attribute of sensitivity) can mitigate this problem.

Secondly, halfway through the practice session, most people discover one side of their jaw muscle suffering a terrible cramp. When this happens, roll the face to engage the incisors on the opposite side.

The more times you practice this drill and the better your body mechanics become at tearing (small circular bites), the faster you will be able to gnaw through the beef. In the beginning, it may take you two or three minutes to get through the meat.

After 20 or 30 pot roasts (and many barbecues!), you will find you can tear your way through the average five-pound slab of meat in seconds.

The next point is the single most-important concept of Kina Mutay: Biting someone "uninterrupted."

To help define uninterrupted biting, picture having your opponent in a bear hug with your arms wrapped around his torso or imagine the opponent in your guard and your arms in a vice grip around his neck while biting his throat.

If you do not have a firm grip on the opponent while biting, his visceral response will be to simply pull away. The result will be a small puncture on the opponent that will hardly do the damage that we require.

Applying this vice grip while making the small tears with the incisors gives us the ability to hang on and bite the assailant until next leap year!

WHERE TO BITE

This brings us to the next principle: Where to bite. Yes, you can use your teeth just about anywhere on an opponent's body, but to bite uninterrupted you must target specific areas. What constitutes a "good" area to bite? We have two criteria to determine this:

1. It should be extremely sensitive to pain. The cheek, neck, ear, nipple area, latissimus dorsi (muscle of the back, found just below the armpit) and the groin are all extremely sensitive regions with many nerve endings.

2. It should be an area that allows you to position yourself so your opponent cannot counter your bite by pulling away or pushing you off. The importance of biting a sensitive area while hanging on cannot be overstated. Using some basic positions in jiu-jitsu, we will present just a few of the many possible bites:

a. You are in the top position, mounted: You can bite the face and neck.

b. You are cross-side on your opponent: From here you can bite the cheek, ear or neck.

c. In the north-south position: You have the groin bite.

d. You have the opponent in your guard: Target the cheek, ear, or neck.

e. You are in your opponent's guard: You have the nipple bite.

f. You are on the bottom and your opponent is cross-side: You can bite the lat muscle if his elbow is across your body or his neck if his elbow is elsewhere.

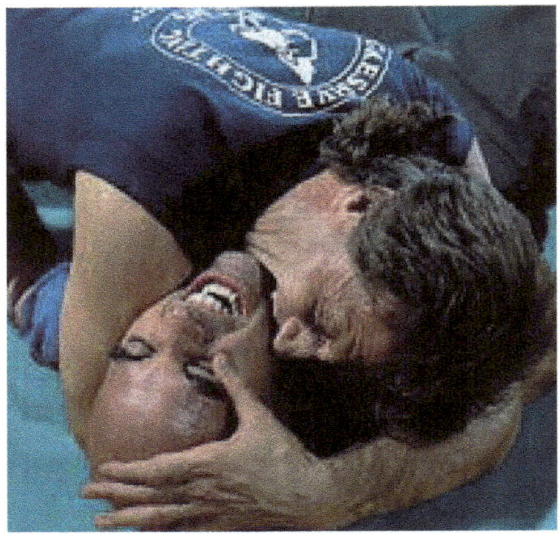

Remember, the key is to hold your opponent so you can bite as long as you want.

His visceral response will be to get the source of his pain (your teeth) away from his body as quickly as possible! Thus, he will try to pull away or push you off, depending on your position, which creates space between his body and yours.

You then can take advantage of this space and push or kick him off. This is the fastest way to get out from under him if you are pinned underneath someone much stronger and heavier than you.

If, however, you fail to hang on to your opponent while you bite, you are not biting uninterrupted. Your opponent will be able to pull away before your bite causes the damage required to get the reaction you need.

WHEN TO BITE

Now we come to Kina Mutay's most-significant training drill. Once you understand the concept of uninterrupted biting and how to use small circular tears to inflict maximum damage, it's time to institute Kina Mutay in actual sparring.

We have illustrated the basics of how and where to bite. The following drill will help you learn when to bite.

Start by rolling on the mat and doing a typical jiu-jitsu practice session. While grappling, begin seeking the appropriate areas of the body to bite (we call this target acquisition).

This process could take anywhere from one second to five minutes. Timing is critical. Only by actually rolling will you develop the proper timing to engage in Kina Mutay at will.

Once you have selected the target area, your next step is to hold your training partner as firmly as you can (grab your own wrist to strengthen the hold). This ensures that your bite will be uninterrupted.

Now simulate the bite by pressing your face firmly against the target as long as possible. The moment your training partner feels the vice grip/bite applied, he should instantly attempt any possible defense (e.g., pushing your face away, breaking the hold, etc.).

If your technique is applied correctly, it should take your partner at least ten seconds to escape the "bite."

The second half of our Kina Mutay equation is the (uninterrupted) eye gouge. To train the eye gouge use the exact same methodology - first wrestle slowly seeking target acquisition.

Each of the positions advantageous for the bite also works well for the eye gouge, with the exception of north-south.

Grab your opponent's neck in your vice grip and gently press on the eyeball until your opponent pulls your hand away. As you get better at eye gouging, have your training partner wear swim goggles and practice the eye gouge more aggressively.

One often overlooked point of Kina Mutay is the tremendous psychological damage a vicious bite or eye gouge will inflict on attacker. When you bite someone, you cause pain. When you bite uninterrupted so your assailant can't stop what you're doing, you create panic.

Add to this that you are biting in a sensitive area (both physically and emotionally) and you are in essence destroying him emotionally - completely demoralizing him.

Using Kina Mutay is an absolute last resort. In this day and age, the thought of having somebody's blood in your mouth is certainly objectionable.

However, in a life-or-death situation - perhaps in an alley while pinned on the ground - implementing a bite could be what creates enough space to shed an attacker so you can get to your feet and escape.

There must be a clear distinction in the martial arts between self-preservation (doing whatever it takes to save yourself and your loved ones) and self-perfection (the sport and training of martial arts).

When we think about bludgeoning somebody with a stick, stabbing him with a knife, or biting a hole in someone's face, the subject is quite distasteful (pardon the pun). However, when protecting yourself or the lives of your loved ones, a simple question begs just one answer:

Is there anything you wouldn't do?

Chapter 12: Edged Weapon Defense

Never has so much been said and written about a subject of which people know so little.

Of all the possible topics an instructor could choose (whether unintentionally or not) in which to misinform students, defense against the knife is by far the most dangerous.

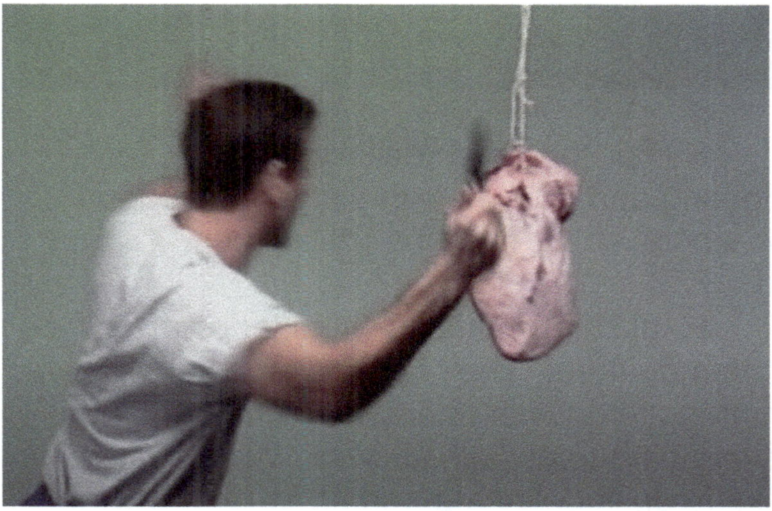

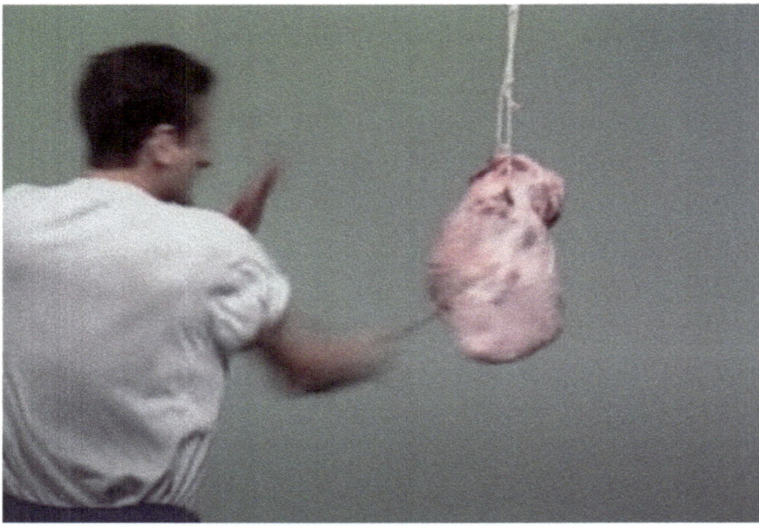

By far, the most realistic methods for fighting and training with all types of edged weapons come from the Philippines.

Real confrontations with blades are all too common there. Their fighting techniques have nothing to do with phony heroism and everything to do with survival. What I would like to do is delineate and prioritize a few of their techniques and training methods.

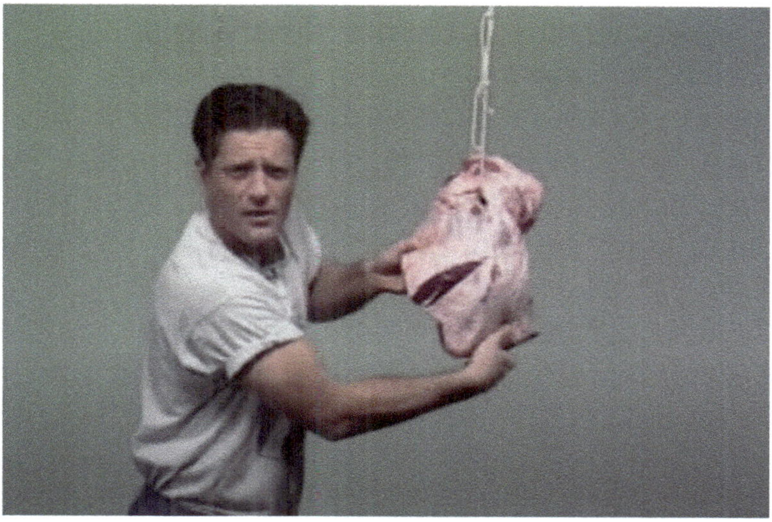

(1) FOOTWORK:

Proper footwork is vital to knife fighting.

Footwork allows us to maintain the correct distance between our opponent and ourselves. Having a low stance with no footwork in this arena is like having a Ferrari with no wheels. We need to move quickly toward, or away from, our opponent.

When an attacker has a knife, the necessity for good footwork is tripled. But what is the proper footwork?

When we think of good footwork in the realm of boxing, almost instantly we picture Muhammad Ali or Sugar Ray Leonard.

The way these boxers move - light, catlike, sticking and moving - is real knife fighting footwork! When you have a razor-sharp knife in your hand, it is fairly obvious that you do not need to plant your feet to do damage to your opponent.

Of course, if you are punching and kicking, it behooves you to get lower and load up for delivering combinations.

However, in a knife fight, it is far more important to stay as light and as agile as possible. One razor slice across the knife hand or one quick thrust directly in the face may be all it takes to end the altercation.

So, remember, when a knife is in the hand, get up on your toes and move.

(2) DISTANCING:

The distance at which we choose to fight our opponent is one of the most important points relative to winning the altercation.

In almost every article, video, or seminar I have seen, the instructor has his students knife fighting in boxing range; that is, close enough for the students to exchange punches.

There are literally hundreds of drills that involve close-quarter knife and stickwork, however, these drills were developed to improve one's attributes, such as sensitivity, coordination and body mechanics.

We call this self-perfection. This should not be confused with real weapons fighting for self-preservation. This is why in real combat, experienced knife fighters always fight outside of kicking range.

The reason is twofold: First, with proper distance, he can more easily avoid being sliced, and secondly, his primary objective is cutting his opponent's knife hand, which is also called ...

(3) DE-FANGING THE SNAKE:

If you can cut the opponent's hand there will be an instant disarm. It is a physical impossibility to hold a knife when the tendons, muscles and ligaments responsible for movement of the hand are severed.

Once you have de-fanged the snake, the snake is harmless and you are now given the choice to kill it or let it go.

Using both correct footwork and maintaining the proper distance from an opponent are crucial to de-tanging the snake.

This same principle also applies to stick fighting. In most modern-day stick tournaments, we see protective headgear on the fighters who are mostly headhunting.

Putting on a helmet and going all-out teaches students how to deal with adrenaline and is certainly a worthwhile experience. This type of practice should constitute about five percent of your training.

Also remember to wear protection on the hands and don't ignore the hand smash! In a tournament, we can witness up to 20 hand smashes without a single point being awarded. Yet, when contact to the head is made, points are given.

This is simply unrealistic. Generally, in stick tournaments, the participants use rattan sticks. The rattan sticks have air going through them; they are considered practice weapons.

If stick fighters used no protection for their hands (as in a real fight) and were using real pieces of oval or hexagonal oak or other hardwood, or perhaps using real pieces of lead pipe, any of those neglected hand smashes would shatter every bone in the opponent's hand!

Although from a sport viewpoint these types of matches are very entertaining, compared to real combat they are akin to having a pillow fight.

(4) TIMING:

A sense of timing is equally as important as the attributes of footwork and distancing, although it is certainly more ambiguous and difficult to explain. Timing can be thought of as hitting your opponent either before, during, or after he takes a shot at you.

Timing is much more of a "heady" game. You must feel that split-second opening for your shot. When one has an expert sense of timing, he can literally move at one-tenth speed and still connect.

I have been hit ten-to-one by old Filipino guys in their 70s. To develop impeccable timing, one needs awareness and line familiarization. These are attributes, which tend to improve with age and experience.

After sparring briefly with Cacoy Canete, who at age 65 basically used my body for target practice, I asked him (while rubbing my welts) at what age was he in his prime. His response was, "In about another ten or 15 years!"

Now let's talk about the relatively less-important points of knife fighting. As with most things in life, perception is everything.

If you perceive the three points mentioned earlier to be the most important points in knife fighting, you will be concentrating on the finger and missing "all the Heavenly glory" (to paraphrase Bruce Lee).

So, what should you do if you are actually attacked by someone with a knife? First, try to run like Carl Lewis! It has been said that to defend yourself against the blade, you must first learn to fight with the blade.

The more you understand the concepts behind fighting with a knife, the more you respect the awesome damage it can inflict.

Unlike a punch or a kick, all the blade has to do is make contact. The attacker does not even have to be particularly skilled with a knife to seriously hurt you.

A very simple acid test demonstrates what will not work: Go to the store and buy an industrial-strength, extra-large red marker.

Find a confined area and instruct a friend to assault you full speed as though the marker were a live blade (not "locking out" any strikes, just slicing and thrusting quickly).

Now, try to apply any blocking or disarming techniques. You will find that you will finish this drill with red lines slashed all over your body!

This graphic illustration will hopefully persuade you that running remains the best option. But suppose there is no avenue of escape. Perhaps you are in a crowded restaurant with your family or in a fenced-in area. Option two is for you to find an equalizer.

A good first reaction would be to grab a knife if you happen to have one or you could pick up a bottle to hold the attacker at bay.

Projectile weapons are great equalizers - pool balls, a chair, a table, pool cues, hot soup in the guy's face - anything to distract this person so you can safely escape.

Finally, we must discuss one final possibility: You are confronted by an angry person with a razor, there is nowhere to run, and there are no equalizers available. (You are in a handball court with Freddie Krueger guarding the exit!)

Personally, I would probably try my odds with a very low and well-timed double-leg takedown, then smother the attacker and simultaneously engage in Kina Mutay.

Even though this strategy may be the most viable, the reality is that I will still be cut by the knife, perhaps fatally. Again, my response of choice when confronted by a blade is to run.

There are many reasons to develop your skill as a knife fighter. Training with a blade is one of the best ways to improve many of the attributes that help you as a martial artist.

In terms of self-preservation in an edged weapon attack, you should concentrate your training on the four most important points of knife fighting:

1. FOOTWORK - Light, loose, and up on your toes (like a boxer).

2. DISTANCE - Largo mano range (past kicking range).

3. DE-FANGING THE SNAKE - Make the opponent's knife hand your primary target.

4. TIMING - Flight time, flight time, and more flight time!

Closing

I hope you enjoyed this book. I know I covered a lot of material. It contains my life's work and I spent over 40 years figuring out what works and what doesn't work. (And I have the scars to prove it.)

If you are interested in more training, if you need any help, or if you'd like to become a certified R.A.T. (Rapid Assault Tactics) instructor, I can be reached at www.FastAndDeadly.com.

Thank you!

About the Author

Paul Vunak has been called "the world's most dangerous man" by Black Belt Magazine. He was personally trained by Dan Inosanto who trained with Bruce Lee. Paul has trained the Navy SEALs, FBI, DEA and numerous other government agencies.

Resources

Here are some additional top selling survival and self-defense books for you…

The Patriot's Guide to (Legally) Hiding Your Guns From the Government... So They Don't Know They Exist and Can Never Confiscate Them

Get the book at **www.SpiesHideGuns.com**

Blade Warrior: Self-Defense Secrets of a Pirate Hunter

Get the book at **www.RomanianRambo.com**

The Escape Bag Blueprint: 37 Items You Must Have to Survive a Crisis.

Get the book at **www.Free37Secrets.com**

Alone and Unafraid: Patriot Defense and Survival Guide

Get the book at **www.FreeWarriorBook.com**

Sleeper Cell Secrets of Spies and Our Founding Fathers. (How to stop socialism)

Get the book at
www.PatriotSleeperCell.com

Milton Keynes UK
Ingram Content Group UK Ltd.
UKHW050615181124
2908UKWH00001B/2

9 781998 050239